A New American House

Architectural Design Competition 1984

Catalogue of Winning and Select Designs

Preface

America has become a country of non-traditional households, where pluralism is increasing and the housing needs of specific constituencies need thoughtful consideration and discussion. "A New American House," the recently concluded national architectural design competition, was organized to explore the needs of non-traditional, professional households in architectural terms.

Three ideas defined the competition: The dramatic change in the number of households not made up of the nuclear family, the rising cost of housing, and the need or desire many more people now have to work at home. From these came the challenge of "A New American House" to design an efficient housing unit, not to exceed 1,000 square feet in area, which would function both as the residence and principal professional workplace for at least one of its occupants. The individual unit served as the basic module for six units on the site in Minneapolis' Whittier neighborhood.

The eighteen award winning designs presented here were selected from 346 entries by a jury consisting of Michael Brill (President, BOSTI, Inc., Buffalo, NY and Professor of Architecture, S.U.N.Y. at Buffalo), Thomas H. Hodne, Jr., FAIA, AICP (President, Thomas Hodne Architects Inc., Minneapolis, MN and Professor and Head, School of Architecture, University of Manitoba, Winnipeg), David Stea (Distinguished Professor of Architecture, University of Wisconsin, Cynthia Weese, AIA (Principal, Weese Hickey Weese Architects, Ltd., Chicago, IL), and James

Wines (President, SITE Projects, Inc., New York, NY and Chairman, Department of Environmental and Interior Design, Parsons School of Design, New York, NY). The select entries presented are representative, exemplary designs.

I would like to thank the members of the advisory panel to "A New American House": Rodney D. Hardy, Brad Hokanson, AIA, Kent W. Robbins, G. Richard Slade, and Milo H. Thompson, AIA; Jeffrey E. Ollswang, AIA, Professional Advisor; Lawrence P. Witzling, Ph.D. and Gerald Weisman, Ph.D. for technical assistance; Dolores Hayden, Professor of Urban Planning at UCLA; Professor Hazel Gamec and students, Scott Makela, Roberta Stege, and Mike Richie, for the graphic design and Steve VanderMeer for the cover photograph of this catalogue; Ruth Dean for the graphic design of the competition program; Madsen & Kuester, Inc. for the graphic design of the competition poster; Patrick Whitney, Peggy Davies, and Patricia H. Brooks for project development; Elizabeth Spring for publicity; and Gisela Erickson and Darlene Olson for administrative assistance.

Harvey Sherman
Competition Director

Catalogue Essay

Economic and demographic patterns are transforming the American family. Over half of all women are in the paid labor force. The dominant family type is the two-earner family. The fastest increasing family type is the single parent family, and single people living alone account for almost a quarter of all households.

To translate changes in family types to changes in housing types is no simple matter. Designers, planners, developers, and mortgage bankers want to innovate, but in what direction does creativity lie? One logical response to women's paid employment is to integrate child care with housing. Another is to promote the development of jobs in residential neighborhoods. Both run counter to traditional practices in zoning and lending. At some future time the United States may be able to unite housing and jobs in residential areas with infant care, day care, and after school care provided as a matter of national policy. In the meantime more informal approaches are necessary.

The "New American House" competition asked architects and planners to explore some of these alternatives, to design ways for employed parents -- men and women -- to undertake paid work at home. It also provided an opportunity for some designers to make housing units suitable for private, licensed child care providers. For these two reasons, the competition's results will appeal to families where parents are both nurturers and earners.

The director of the competition, Harvey Sherman, a single parent himself, can be seen as one of many activists concerned about architectural solutions to changing family forms in the twentieth century. As early as 1898, Charlotte Perkins Gilman wrote in *Women and Economics* that any designer who could create an apartment hotel with full child care for employed mothers would find it to be one of "the biggest businesses on earth." During World War II many of the ideas proposed by Gilman and her successors became reality in the housing built for the Rosie the Riveter families at Vanport City, Oregon, in 1943. But the suburban boom of the postwar era eroded these gains. By the 1950s and 1960s, most public housing was built without any thought for day care or job training, even though single parent mothers usually constituted the majority of tenants. Suburban neighborhoods were no better.

The "New American House" competition clearly stated that in 1984, there is a "need for new house forms which have the ability to provide not only the domestic setting for non-traditional households, but also the professional setting for those who need, or desire, to work at home." Competitors had to place six units combining home and office on a site of a little less than half an acre in the Whittier neighborhood in Minneapolis. From among 346 entrants, three winners were chosen. All three attempted to integrate their designs into a streetscape of one and two family houses. All gave architectural expression to the work space as well as the domestic space to create a new residential type.

The winners of the prize for best design, Troy West and Jacqueline Leavitt, placed the six office spaces on the major street, with row houses behind. Jill Stoner, second prize winner, moved the offices to one edge of the site with the housing above. Carlo Pelliccia, winner of the third prize, produced a dense urban scheme with six offices along two central pedestrian paths, and three units on each side opposite the offices.

Michael Brill, one of the jury members, noted these three solutions suggest "a new typology" because the designers faced the tension between work and home, and expressed it by looking for "an aesthetic which comes from that tension." Juror David Stea said, "People are understandably timid about it. How do you celebrate the workplace without stigmatizing it?" Given "the mom and pop storefront on the corner," commented Thomas Hodne, "New American House is a revival of an old concept." Yet Cynthia Weese argued, "Working at home is no longer a lonely thing. Here is a community of people working side by side." James Wines argued that the best solutions to this problem are "endlessly readaptive,' and thus, timeless. All the jury members seemed to agree that the competition revealed possibilities for the "more productive use of space," by avoiding the duplication of circulation and amenities that occurs in plans for commercial neighborhoods deserted at night and residential ones empty during the day.

In addition to the three main prizes, Awards of Merit and Honorable Mentions were distributed, and all of these plus a few additional projects are represented in this catalogue. From small towns and major cities, in all regions of the United States, experienced designers as well as talented students directed their energies to this competition. The ingenuity and diversity of their solutions promise new excitement in American housing during the next decade as some of these prototypical solutions are built and tested.

Dolores Hayden
Professor of Urban Planning
University of California, Los Angeles

Troy West
Jacqueline Leavitt

Wakefield, Rhode Island

We have been working on issues about how people function in houses for some time. Four years ago, we turned our attention to the needs of single parents and designed a congregate house, which, after feedback from potential users, was modified to include an accessory apartment for an elderly person. This design won first prize in an exhibition sponsored by California State University's Women's Studies program at Long Beach. We spent considerable time thinking through the issues of providing private as well as shared space, areas for personal use and places where people could earn a living working at home, provisions for child care and for adult socializing, and the connection to outdoor spaces.

In approaching the design for the New American House, we built on our earlier work but followed the competition guidelines quite faithfully. Each of the work spaces is approached from the street. This enables access to activities that are otherwise excluded from or kept hidden in residential neighborhoods. Familiar front yards lead to each work space. A trellis spans the yard to the work space and, in good weather, can be used as an outdoor room. The work space is connected to the house with a spine that is an efficient, linear kitchen. This design creates an enclosed garden that provides a protected outdoor space for children and the constant presence of nature. This closeness to nature is also made possible with a second floor deck overlooking the garden.

Main access to the residence is through the alley. The carport in the rear can be covered with a trellis and plants. The quasi-private space in the rear is a place for teenagers to play and neighbors to get together. The various scenarios detailed on the plan itself show how the units can be arranged flexibly for a variety of households.

The house has a gable roof, which is associated with the classic, single

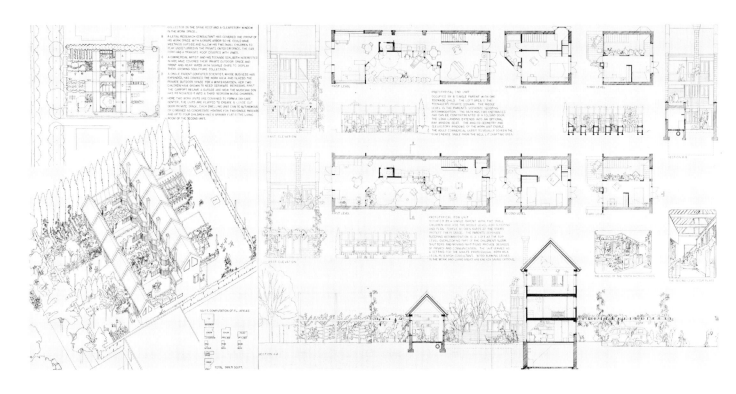

First Place

family home. Though each house stands on its own, the design is best seen as an association of houses that form both a private and community experience for the new American householder. The units can be flipped and combined so work spaces join to provide a child care center, and residential spaces join to accommodate congregate housing. Activities in the work spaces can relate to each other and help provide an urban quality. The front and rear yards can be used in a communal fashion. This design enables people to be by themselves and yet be part of a community.

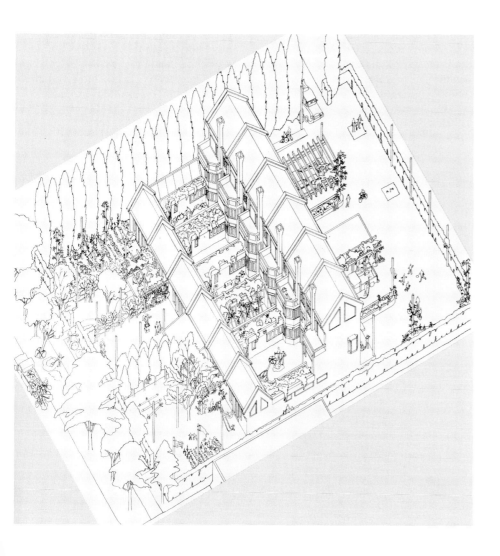

Jill Stoner

Philadelphia, Pennsylvania

The design is a reinterpretation of the traditional notions of house. From Clinton Street we see a singular image of garage, house, and garden. The lower level under the "bridges" leads to shared vestibules to the professional units. The other gate, at the upper garden level, leads to the bridges and to the units' front doors. From the garage, staircases meet these passageways, and front door and back door become one. Chimneys frame this entrance. At the roof, a window is contained within and between the chimneys to light the front and back meeting places from above. The upper garden is shared by all; back courtyards are completely private. Porches at the kitchen level are shared by neighboring units and are anchored to the garage by outdoor cooking hearths.

The traditional party wall has become thick. One wall is carved with such shared functions as the entrance passage, bedroom windows into the light well, and chimney flues for both oil burner and woodstoves. The other wall shares the entrance to the professional spaces, a lavatory, kitchenette, stairs, bath, porch, and all plumbing. Between these two walls is the private space of each house.

Design of the units' interiors varies with the lifestyles and professions of the occupants. Below are several scenarios:

Scenario #1: The Writer. The unit is occupied by a married couple with no children. The husband teaches elementary school, and his wife is an author of children's books. Her professional office has bookcases in the masonry recess, a large writing desk, and a sitting area with woodstove. The first floor is furnished similarly to the first floor in Scenario #5. The top floor is a single bedroom with partitioned dressing area.

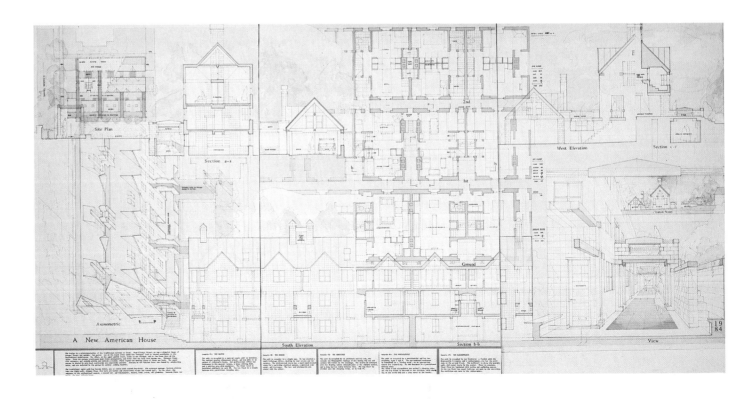

Scenario #2: The Broker. The unit is occupied by a single man. He has started a small brokerage office, dealing in real estate and insurance. The professional space has a small partitioned space for a part-time clerical person, a personal computer, and bookcases. The lavatory and kitchenette are shared with the writer.

Scenario #3: The Architect. The unit is occupied by an architect and his son, who attends the Minneapolis College of Art and Design during the day and assists his father in the evenings. The studio is arranged with two drawing tables perpendicular to the chimney masses and a long lay-out table between them. The top floor is divided into two sleeping rooms, as described in Scenario #5.

Scenario #4: The Psychiatrist. The unit is occupied by a psychiatrist and her two children, ages 4 and 6. The professional workspace is furnished as a "living room," in an appropriate manner for counseling. At the entrance is a partitioned waiting area. The first floor accommodates the mother's sleeping area and the top floor is devoted to the children, with sleeping at the north end and a play space at the south.

Scenario #5: The Cabinetmaker. The unit is occupied by two brothers, a flutist with the Minnesota Orchestra and a cabinetmaker who has his workshop on the ground floor. The workbench is positioned along the masonry wall, with power tools in the center. The floor is concrete. The first floor is furnished with eating and gathering spaces. On the top floor, wardrobes divide the space into two equal bedrooms. The wardrobes are made by the cabinetmaker.

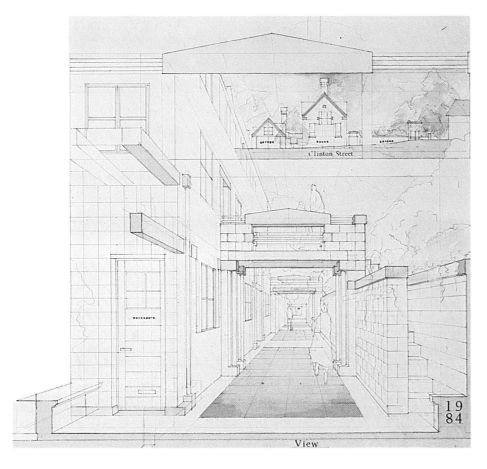

7

Carlo Pelliccia

Charlottesville, Virginia

With the Industrial Revolution and the birth of the contemporary city, human activities became compartmentalized and the city fragmented. This project takes us on a trip into the romantic past of a medieval town. It also conjures a dream of freedom for creative activity in the future. One works where he or she lives, with family or friend. The groups of houses become small "communities," with their own pedestrian streets. The houses are surrounded by gardens and walls which create a sense of community, a sense of neighborhood. Narrow streets give protection against inclement weather but also allow for commerce and encourage human exchange, relationships, friendships. Each unit is a bridgehouse: each provides a link between past and present, between tradition and innovation, between the place of the family and the place of work. In this project the street represents the "city" and the houses embrace it.

Small, private gardens are developed along the site's perimeter. From these gardens, one passes behind the project to a communal garden dominated by a roof terrace that protects the garages. This large community terrace is located a half-level above the houses' main level, with the garages a half-level below the houses. The roofs are oriented north-south, permitting the use of solar panels.

The two narrow pedestrian streets, the skeleton of the system, present an alternation of void and solid, light and shadow, bridge and well, house door and office door. The small windows overlooking the streets foster privacy within the houses. By contrast, the windows facing the private gardens are considerably larger, allowing the inhabitants to think of the garden as an extension of the living room. The internal axis of the houses/studios, oriented north-south, contrasts with the west-east axis of the two pedestrian

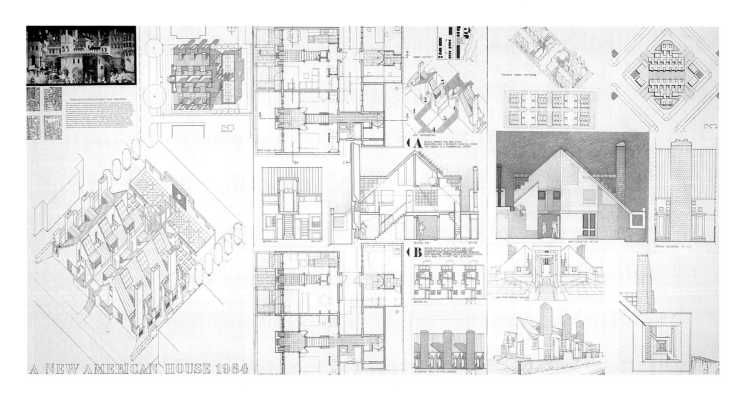

streets. This interwoven web of circulation -- private and public -- is the most important formal characteristic of the project.

The streets originate and end in the entrance gateway, which can assume a variety of forms. Each group of units may express its individuality in a different solution to the entrance.

Within the house, the connecting axis between the studio and the living area becomes a place where events occur. The massive fireplace, violently expressed outside (almost like a medieval tower), becomes a place of relaxation indoors in the small lounge

shared by the two upstairs rooms. The house and the studio doors are aligned on the same axis as the two stairways, one leading straight into the house, the other spiraling into the study. This axis allows two uninterrupted, interior views which are relatively long (34 feet and 37 feet) for a small unit.

The centralization of the island of studios/offices permits space allocation to vary according to the owners' needs. Some owners may choose to share their working space with their neighbors.

The proposed building materials for the project are woodframing, concrete blocks, stucco, and metal roofing.

For urban planning, this project offers important possibilities of "grouping," which the bridge-house allows. Some of these are diagrammatically illustrated. For example, the "linear superblock" with its four service courts and 48 units, may be developed along a linear garden which runs the full length of the block. By contrast, the "square block" lines 16 units with garages on a grid which is rotated 45 degrees away from the city street grid. The corners of the block remain free for such urban uses as shops or small public gardens.

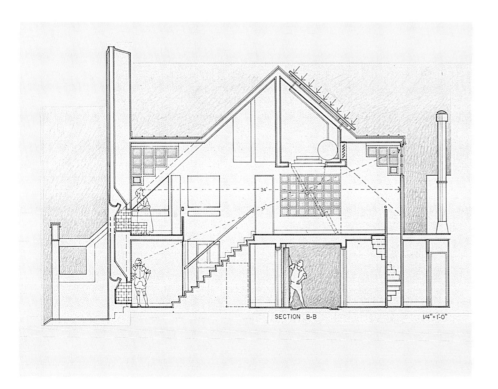

SECTION B-B   1/4"=1'-0"

Bob Burnham
William C. Miller

Virginia Cartwright

Manhattan, Kansas

The architectural resources for making a small dwelling are limited and must be used with considerable care. Small dwellings do not permit extravagent form essays. Instead they require the concentration of spatial impact, the careful definition of inside/outside relationships, and the thoughtful development of details. A complex of units also requires a clear spatial order, careful articulation of edges and surfaces, and incorporation of appropriate energy responses.

Making full use of the small site and explicitly defining public and private realms demand careful arrangement of dwellings and exterior spaces.

Transforming the traditional suburban spatial pattern was the starting point. The pedestrian walkways and small entry courts on the north side of the units are equivalent to streets and front yards; the back yards become defined southern garden spaces. The shaping and massing of the units coupled with the use of gateways, walls, and hedges articulate individual unit identity.

A sense of spaciousness is achieved within the unit by concentrating a large percentage of the floor area in the sitting/dining room. Developed as an expansive space of significant volume with rich edges -- full height bay window, ceramic tile stove, balcony,

and built-in benches -- this room is simultaneously a series of small places for specific activities and a large room or "great hall."

The edges and surfaces of buildings speak strongly to us, for they define spaces and forms; spatial and surface detail establish scale and experiential qualities. The design of the public and private facades of the units reverse the norms found in the traditional suburban house. The detail development of the public face makes use of small scaled, intimate, and casual elements. In contrast, the private face of the garden facade is more formal and monumental in its disposition of elements.

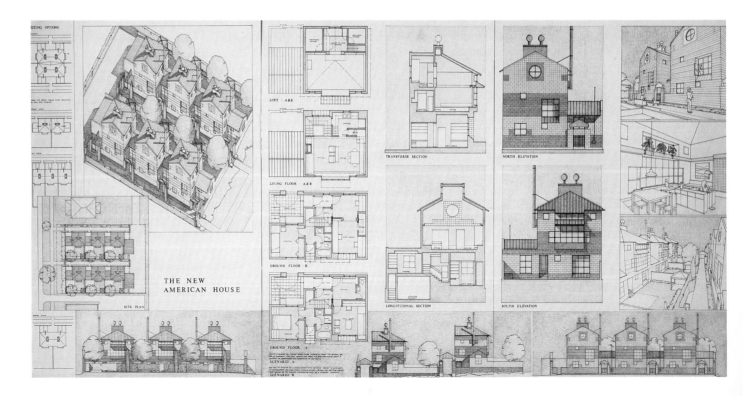

THE NEW AMERICAN HOUSE

Award of Merit

Appropriate energy response in architecture ensures harmony with climate. Energy should be considered equally with other variables in creating quality and enhancement of living. This design uses basic passive architectural strategies, orientation, amount and positioning of glazing, natural ventilation, and material selection to conserve energy. The southern exposure of the private garden maximizes its use as an extension of the interior living spaces.

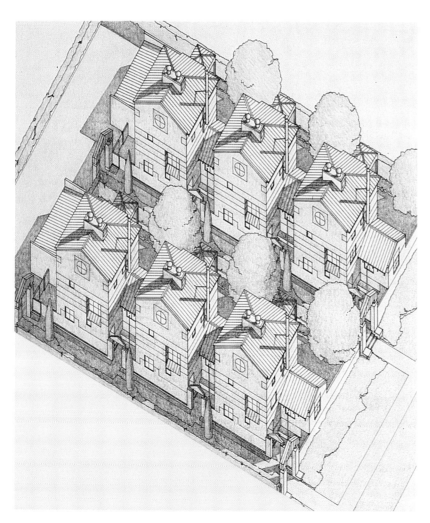

Roger C. Erickson

Boston, Massachusetts

This site plan was approached with three main factors in mind: parking, open spaces, and orientation.

Parking is located on the site's perimeter, in this case to the rear, adjacent to the highway. Both parking and the garage structure provide a visual and sound barrier for the complex as well as additional recreational space for basketball, handball, etc.

Arranged in a hierarchy, open space begins with the neighborhood street and its activities; continues in the front yard setback, which signifies semi-private turf; and includes the interior green, which belongs to the residents and their visitors. The green features such pedestrian amenities as trees, shrubs, flowers, benches, and lighting, and can function as a community meeting place. Directly from the community green, one enters the patio or private outdoor space for each unit. In these spaces, a variety of landscaping treatments can be used, limited only by the imagination of the occupants. Directly from the private patio, one enters the unit and its personalized spaces.

Of all considerations, the sun orientation was probably the most important factor in the site design. All units are oriented to catch maximum sun exposure during the short winter days, when passive solar warmth is needed most. Exterior shades shut out strong, unwanted summer sun. Clerestory windows admit summer breezes as well as more light.

The units are designed to be flexible, yet preserve the separation, both horizontally and vertically, between the living and working areas. Based on a Scandinavian prototype, these patio or atrium houses are perfectly square, with one quarter set aside for a private garden. Such proportions make great flexibility possible in arranging the units

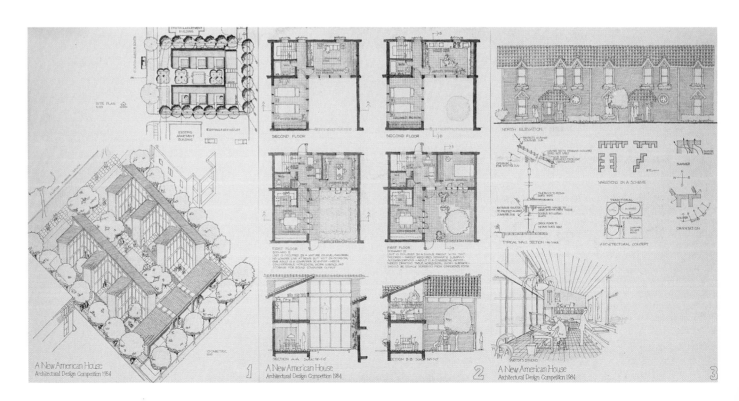

in many different configurations. Each unit can be entered through any of four sides.

The roof angle is determined by the lowest sun angle during the winter months. Tiles serve to "insulate" the roof, provide ventilation, and give a warm, traditional feeling to the complex. The inner court facade

treatment is strictly functional, due to the energy demands; but the exterior is very traditional, designed to blend in with the surrounding neighborhood.

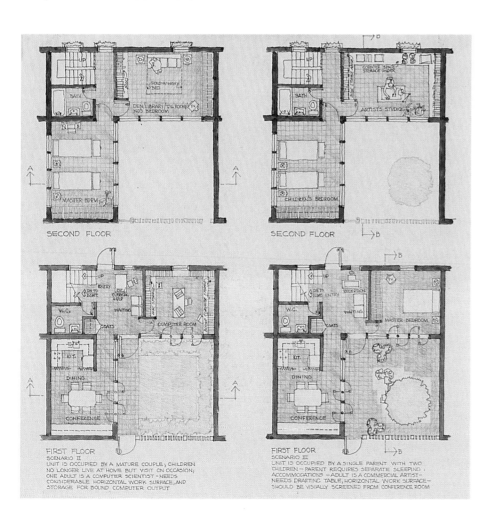

SECOND FLOOR

SECOND FLOOR

FIRST FLOOR
SCENARIO II
UNIT IS OCCUPIED BY A MATURE COUPLE; CHILDREN NO LONGER LIVE AT HOME BUT VISIT ON OCCASION; ONE ADULT IS A COMPUTER SCIENTIST – NEEDS CONSIDERABLE HORIZONTAL WORK SURFACE, AND STORAGE FOR BOUND COMPUTER OUTPUT

FIRST FLOOR
SCENARIO III
UNIT IS OCCUPIED BY A SINGLE PARENT WITH TWO CHILDREN – PARENT REQUIRES SEPARATE SLEEPING ACCOMMODATIONS – ADULT IS A COMMERCIAL ARTIST – NEEDS DRAFTING TABLE, HORIZONTAL WORK SURFACE – SHOULD BE VISUALLY SCREENED FROM CONFERENCE ROOM

Michael Pyatok

Oakland, California

A New American House must demonstrate comfort but consume less land and fewer resources. A small unit footprint (20' x 20') releases valuable urban land which can serve as open space for private, semi-public and public recreation. Consequently, in this design "Minnesota in a microcosm" is created with forest, farm, urban courtyards and backyards in each sample site plan. Parking is not attached to each house, expanding the front and back for public and private uses. Short walks from clustered garages are easy to maintain during winter if equipment is shared by six households. The small footprint allows flexible site planning either to address the street (E,F,G) or retreat to a more private "estate" (A,B,C,D).

Being square, the units can accommodate corner, middle and end locations, minimize wall area for energy efficiency, and minimize corners for ease of construction. The intersecting gable roof economizes on interior volume and also faces roofs in all directions, enhancing solar panel opportunities regardless of where the unit is located. The gable roof also eliminates any gutters and the problem of ice damming. Each house has two porches, one for the public side, one for the private. Sufficient space separates neighboring porches to allow snow from the roof to accumulate on the ground without impeding entry. Domestic and business entries can be designed on one side (A,C,E,F,G) or opposite sides (B,D). When both entries are on one side, they can either be together at the ground floor (C,E) or the domestic entry can ascend optional exterior stairs and enter at the main living level through an air lock (A,F,G).

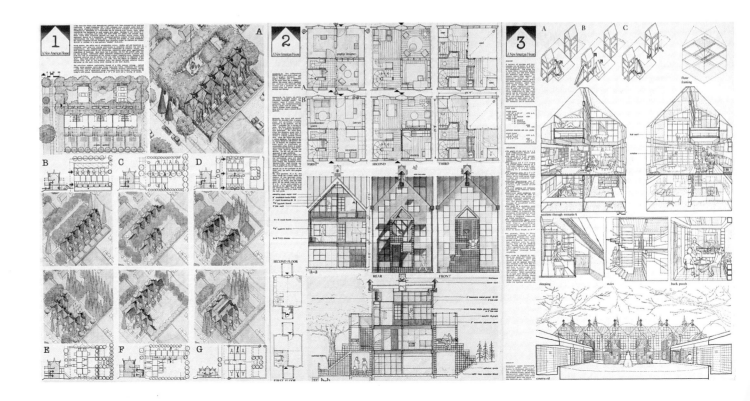

The exteriors combine comfortable images of a 19th century cottage -- gabled roofs, stone porches, stove pipe flues, barn-like vents, whimsical bird houses -- with 20th century life-style demands -- minimum exterior maintenance, energy efficiency, and a panelized image borrowed from the higher technology of today's work place, made residential by a 2' x 2' grid and a variety of colors.

While designed for the Minneapolis climate and working professionals, the house can accommodate lower income households in other regions. The higher priced metal roof and wall panels intended to reduce annoying maintenance for busy upper income professionals can be replaced with less costly composition shingles and stucco while the stone porch could be wood. The first floor could be rented as a studio apartment to supplement the income of a single parent household or a homeowner unexpectedly forced into unemployment. Also, a senior of modest means could own the home, living in the first floor studio while renting the upper 2-bedroom unit. The small, 20' x 20', unit footprint enables the house to be built on infill lots, reducing land costs.

Because the strong roof shape and porch additions connote an archetypal residential character in the U.S., the house can fit into older residential neighborhoods in most cities. In this design, work place meets homestead and country meets city. Victorian verticality, rural barn roof imagery, and domestic flues are mated with mechanistic repetition, metallic precision, and an urban archetypal porch and stoop, in the American way --eclectic.

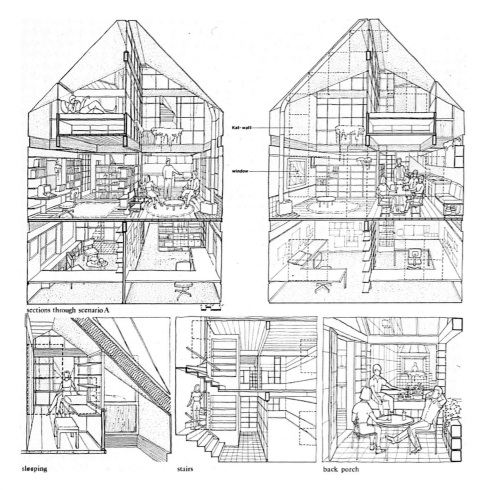

sections through scenario A

sleeping   stairs   back porch

Jeanne Marie Duvall
Rosaria F. Hodgdon

Eugene, Oregon

Honorable Mention

The concepts embodied in this design strive to meet the needs of today's society while reflecting the traditional American ideals of family and home. This project attempts to provide the maximum flexibility and efficiency that is needed by the New American Household.

The facade articulates the individuality of each unit yet unites them all into an harmonious whole. Shared areas between the units maximize space while providing a pleasant transition from the street for the occupants and their guests.

A major concern of this project is the juxtaposition of the workplace and living areas in each unit. A set of special doors that move on tracks make possible a variety of openings, which allow interaction and closure between the living and work areas. The spaces in the unit are very flexible and can accommodate the many different activities that individual households require. Built-in facilities help to maximize space.

The openness of the unit's interior is also found on the site. While the front of the project is more formal and individual, the area in back of the dwellings is more open, creating a mixture of shared and private spaces.

The interior receives light through skylights and areas of glass block. As the sun enters the skylights, it is stored in the brick walls to create a passive solar system. The skylights also function as a cooling system, for they open as a form of stack ventilation.

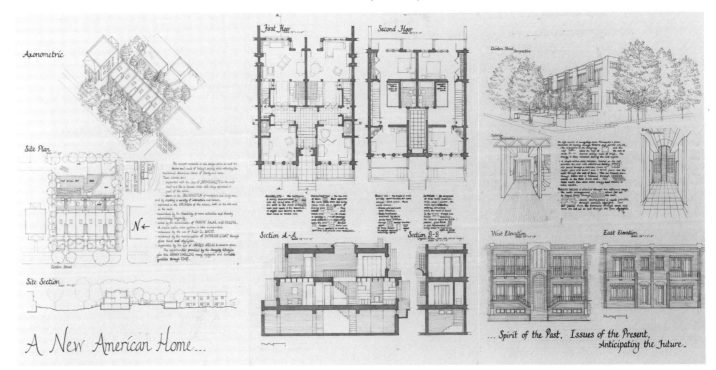

16

William Buckingham
Margery Morgan

Dorchester, Massachusetts

We have had a long-standing interest in the issues the competition posed and are fascinated with the image of "house" in architectural theory and popular culture. In developing our version of "A New American House," we focused on three issues: integrating the houses into a residential neighborhood, planning thoroughly practical dwellings, and creating a strong sense of "houseness," that was consonant with the prototypical aspect of the competition program.

In response to the character of the neighborhood, we placed two groups of three houses perpendicular to the street, with their gable ends echoing the profile of the Victorian houses nearby. A central driveway leads to garages and "professional" entries; footpaths at the sides of the site lead to garden gates and "family" entries. Shared service facilities and storage space are located in a small pavilion which terminates the view down the central drive and conceals the expressway beyond.

We planned the houses on two stories. The entries, professional work space, and garage are on the first floor; purely domestic spaces are on the second. The upper floor has a quiet end (bedrooms and baths) and an active end (living and dining areas and kitchen). On both floors the principal room extends through the house, with windows on both ends. Thus, these rooms are well lit, regardless of the orientation of the house. We have used different ceiling heights, varied window types, and built-in storage to give visual interest to rooms that have no wasted space. Since some residents will spend twenty-four hours a day within these walls, a variety of aesthetic experiences is particularly important.

On the exterior, we expressed the functional division of each dwelling into professional and private spaces by a change of materials from brick below to shingles above. This style can be characterized simply as "domestic," with sheltering roofs a dominant theme. It blends easily with a variety of late 19th and 20th century houses. We are convinced, on the basis of research as well as intuition, that people who need dwellings organized in a novel way nevertheless prefer that their houses be comfortably familiar in appearance. Our goal was to produce a group of houses that would be both novel and familiar, responding to the widely-felt needs for continuity and for change.

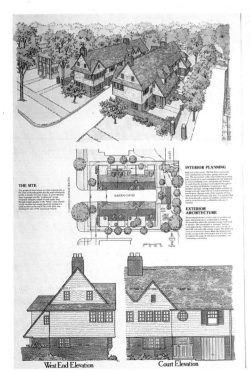

THE SITE

INTERIOR PLANNING

EXTERIOR ARCHITECTURE

West End Elevation

Court Elevation

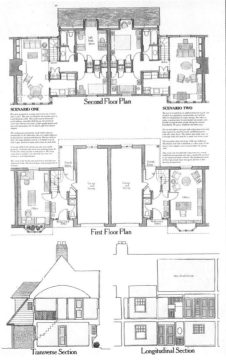

Second Floor Plan

SCENARIO ONE

SCENARIO TWO

First Floor Plan

Transverse Section

Longitudinal Section

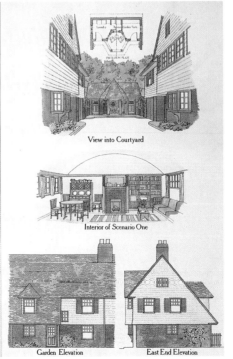

View into Courtyard

Interior of Scenario One

Garden Elevation

East End Elevation

Norman Crowe

Southbend, Indiana

These buildings recall commodious houses of turn-of-the-century American neighborhoods. Gable roofs, divided windows, generous overhangs, symmetrical elements, and dormers combine with predominant horizontal lines on the entrance elevations to create a relaxed character and integrate the units into the neighborhood.

A group of units functions as a mini-community, with shared outdoor spaces and a common architectural expression for the entire group. Within the enclosed yard or within each unit itself, privacy and the identity of the individual unit are accentuated.

The private enclosed yards and the rooms adjacent to them form an ensemble for daily living. The entrance vestibule and stairs to the office or studio lie outside that ensemble, insuring separation and identity of the professional work area from the living areas. The gate to each yard provides a casual entry to the unit, especially in warm seasons. The formal, main entrance to the living unit is located in a vestibule, with an internal stair to the office/studio.

The narrow design of the building maximizes southern exposure and enables the site to be zoned into successive "layers" of public to private domains. First are public domains (walkways and common squares), then semi-public (front porches and entrances to the professional offices/studios), then semi-private (front yards of each unit), and, finally, private domains (interiors of the units). The buildings always face south, and may be built into configurations appropriate for north-south or east-west streets, and north sloping, south sloping, or flat sites, as shown on the drawings.

All rooms except toilet rooms and baths face south, providing continuous access to winter sun, while overhangs are designed to eliminate the penetration of summer sun. The high roof maximizes surfaces available to solar collectors, shown here as both passive (below) and active (above) types. The north wall has no openings except for ventilation and a skylight effect. This decreases heat loss and insures privacy for the adjacent units.

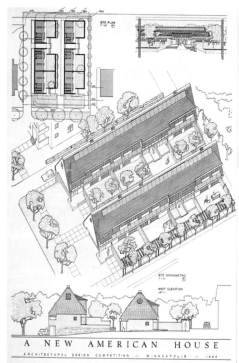

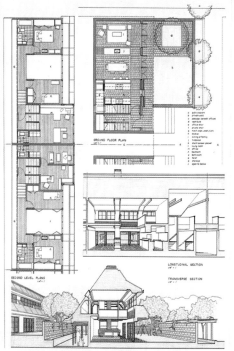

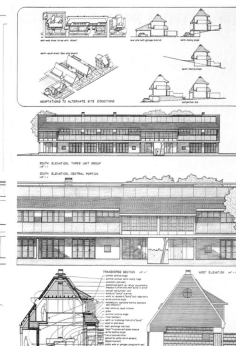

Daryl E. Hansen

Minneapolis, Minnesota

A major objective in the design of this "New American House" prototype is to establish flexible space planning "zones" and a framework that allow residents to embellish, use, and change spaces according to their own tastes and lifestyles and to vary unit appearance. Options include plan configuration, extent of partitioning and use of moving partitions, facade treatment, roof form, use of attic expansion, attached garage (different site), energy conscious measures, balconies, solarium, extent of "fixed" support areas, and aesthetic choices.

The site is divided into public and private zones. The center public zone provides access to the offices. Activities and amenities in this zone would be decided by the residential group, relative to cost and degree of development over time. The group would also choose the wood lath forms shown and the site features. The private zone includes the main entry to the living portion of each unit and private outdoor space. Both private and public zones have easily observable access from the street and parking area.

The unit itself consists of four, flexible living and working area modules. These four symmetrical squares can be reversed in two directions as well as between floors. Fixed vertical circulation, entry areas, and hygiene modules are symmetrically arranged around the four squares for increased flexibility. Support zones attached to each of the four modules may be used for fixed storage, overhang and shading options, energy conservation measures, or horizontal expansion.

The roof form is also flexible and can rotate or change shape for favorable solar orientation with respect to site constraints. The roof space may be used for storage or future expansion by extending the stair vertically within its zone.

Corner window arrangements for the four square modules can accommodate varying common wall conditions with the use of ventilation/light wells. Units may be grouped in a variety of site configurations. These principles are demonstrated in the four and six-unit atrium plans.

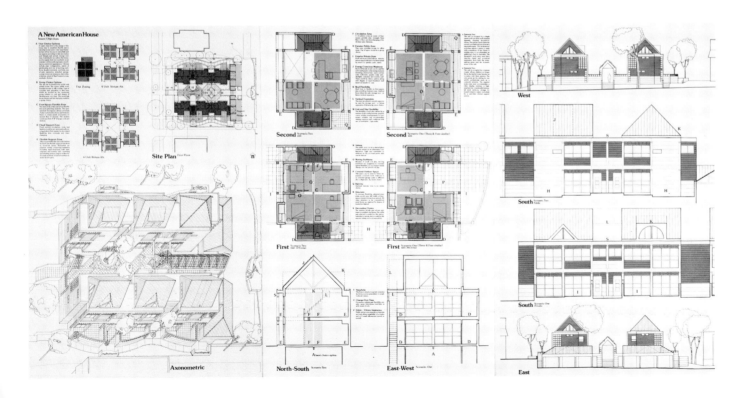

Thomas A. Forman
Rick J. Lukasik

The form of the American home has been shaped through time by ambitions, indulgences and inspirations.

We have asked it to be a place of illusion, a cottage. We asked it to provide for ease of living, become a machine. We changed its role from housing families to sheltering individuals. We have used it as a place of refuge while risking self-expression in our choice of homes. We have changed the form of the house to meet the perception of changed times.

The new American home is a place for each of us to express our own particular ambitions and indulgences.

Steven Zebich

Chicago, Illinois

We want to inspire the Anyone/Anywhere Home.

Anyone: Let's be able to change the place we live without changing places. Our home should adapt to life.

Anywhere: Live and work at one place. Everyone will have a well-defined and equipped space from which to form varied "scales" of collective situations.

We have proposed a home framework that recognizes the American fear of and fascination with the conflict between technology and tradition. The home will allow for human expression of traditions while using technological potential -- a Home of Positive Energy

that sets a course for the future while maintaining a continuing tradition.

Communication will soon replace transportation. The mobility of mind rather than body will provide for maximum opportunities at a minimum risk.

The Home will reach out to the world to communicate, to form communities. The world is in your window; any number of houses will form a community.

Nothing is really new. An evolutionary response to the time is always needed. The Victorian Cottage. The tract house. Now, the Anyone/Anywhere House is that response.

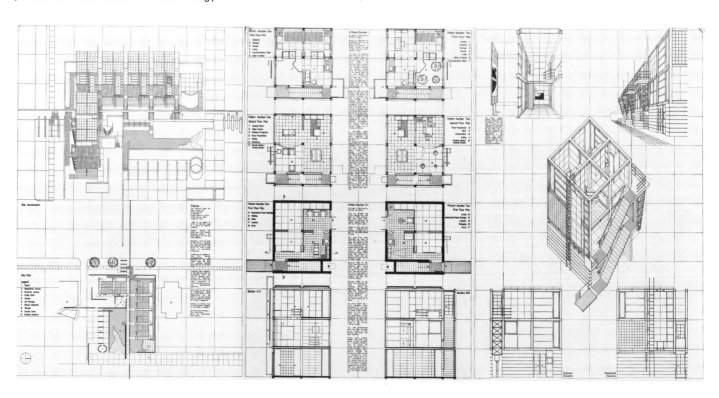

Dennis W. Grebner

St. Paul, Minnesota

Because of my concern for "public space" and the need to fit houses into their surroundings, I felt it necessary to use an arrangement of dwelling units that gave a strong edge, a street facade to the public side. Hence, the six units are ranked across the width of the property.

The basic unit plan and dwelling/garden arrangement use as a source the nineteenth century English terrace house. The exterior form draws upon the aesthetic of the "Herrenhuis" (Burgher houses) of seventeenth century Amsterdam. The language of forms, the simplified Baroque stepped gables at the ends, the modified classical molding configurations, and the "small paned" windows are all borrowed from other times because of their beauty and expression of feeling.

A small, paved garden area at each unit's front entry is separated from the public walk by a slight grade change and a low decorative fence. This area provides a transition between the house and the street, contributing to the ceremony of arrival/entry and giving the resident a place from which to "watch the world go by." The courtyard/garden and the sundeck over the garage are private outdoor spaces for gardening, sitting, playing, and enjoying nature in the city.

Each unit is given a sense of identity through individually designed "totem" latticed cages which can support plants. Entry into the business place and dwelling are clearly separated by the split level design, with stairs leading up to the house and down to the office.

This design permits residents to expand and change their units economically. Interior partitions are non-load bearing, and the insulated, exterior wall cladding on the rear facade is removable and reusable. There is room for additions to the dwelling on the courtyard side. A "mother-in-law" apartment can be added over the garage for future income potential or to accommodate a life style change. The garage can also be screened in to serve as an alternative living space in the summer. The "quintessential Minnesota basement" provides residents with low cost space for rough use, storage, utilities, heating equipment, and workshop.

Finally, super insulation, natural ventilation through recirculation, solar access in winter for passive heating, and solar shading in summer for cooling are natural environmental conditioning features which reduce the use of costly resources to provide environmental comfort.

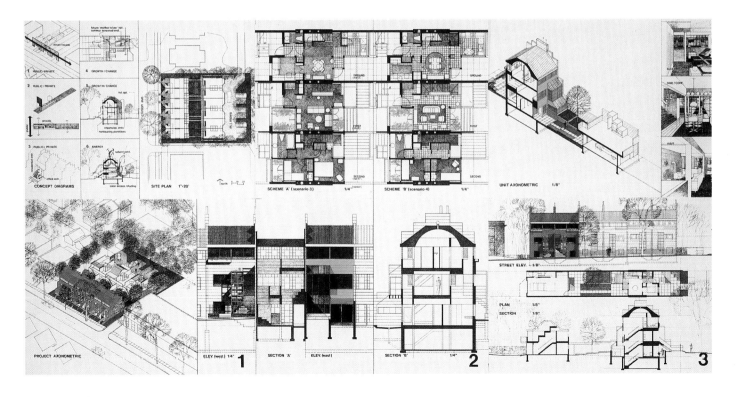

Kenneth Brown
Edward Papp

Arlington, Virginia

Given the limitations of arranging six units on this site, our intention was to design a visually prominent unit cluster in relation to adjacent buildings, to articulate each individual unit within the cluster, and to give a clear sense of identity to the professional work-place and entry of each unit. The forms and massing of the six unit cluster, attached garages, and courtyard enclosures correspond to the forms of two and three story detached houses, townhouses, and apartment buildings present in the immediate neighborhood.

Each unit is composed of a main, multi-story mass, a one story projection facing the pedestrian mews, and a courtyard enclosure. The one story projection recalls the American "storefront" while retaining the gable form of the larger mass, which contains the unit's domestic spaces on two levels. A prominent roof monitor allows ventilation of and permits light penetration into the interior spaces.

The unit plan responds to the diverse functional and behavioral aspects of professional lifestyles while creating a comfortable and flexible living environment for its inhabitants. The

entertainment, dining, and work activities are located on the lower level and relate directly to adjacent, outdoor courtyard spaces. The sleeping areas are situated on the upper level, affording the occupants their needed privacy. The multi-story central space is dominated by a thermal and service wall, providing passive solar capabilities and enhancing vertical circulation within the unit. Both volume and the wall penetrations within this space physically extend the adjoining living and sleeping areas.

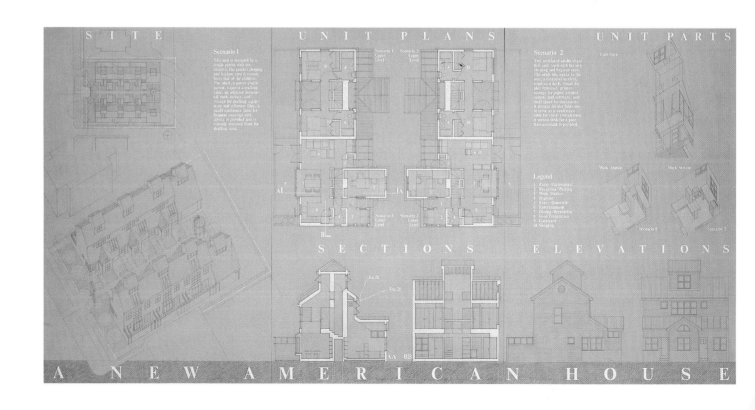

Gene Ernst
Carsten Jensen

Gwen Owens-Wilson

Manhattan, Kansas

Winter Garden is an assembly of six, 24-foot units. Each has an entry court on grade level, with an overlooking conservatory on a second level deck. Units can be assembled in groupings of two or three on small infill lots or in larger configurations, such as Winter Garden. The units share a common glazed gallery, which serves as a spatial extension of the entry courts and conservatories. This entire area can be filled with vegetation to provide usable outdoor space year around in northern locations such as Minneapolis. The gallery space is not conditioned, but depends upon passive solar gain and unit heat loss in the winter, and cooling

winds in the summer, which enter through a pivoted sash.

Entry courts provide separate access to office and living areas. The living space on each unit's second level extends both visually and physically to the conservatory deck. By adding a glazed partition between the conservatory deck and the upper volume of the entry court, the living area can be opened to the deck without regard to season.

Within each unit, load-bearing party walls carry the clear span floor structure. This design allows occupants to determine interior partition locations, offering the freedom to change

relatively easily. Thus, the living and food preparation areas on grade can be interchanged with the sleeping areas on the second level. Perimeter and party walls are constructed of masonry with a stucco finish to provide thermal mass for passive solar storage.

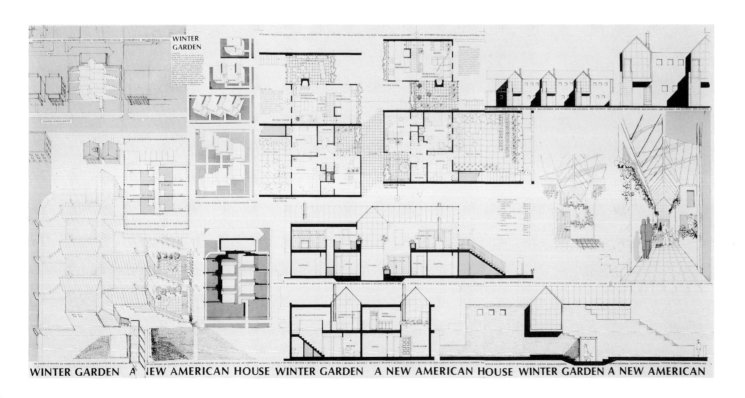

WINTER GARDEN A NEW AMERICAN HOUSE WINTER GARDEN A NEW AMERICAN HOUSE WINTER GARDEN A NEW AMERICAN

James Stacy Norris

Pocasset, Massachusetts

A non-traditional home should provide the amenities of the typical single family home and respect the need for privacy. Such privacy should be maintained not only between office and home, but also between the inhabitants living within the residence. To accomplish this, the office must be visually and physically distinct from the living area, while the spaces within the living area must be physically separate from each other. In this design, the offices are located directly off the street for public visibility as well as accessibility. The living areas are set back and behind the offices, providing a clear distinction between the public and private realms.

The living areas are organized around an interior courtyard, which physically separates the rooms so the occupants may carry on different activities in complete privacy. Located in the courtyard, the stairs lead to rooms placed at each half level. The rooms are simply stair landings; as one ascends the stairs, the space becomes more private.

From the courtyard, light and ventilation come into the center of the house. In a sense, the courtyard is an "air plenum" which allows the air to circulate through the rooms. Air movement is assisted by a fan located in the louvered service space. The use of glass block for the courtyard wall serves a dual function: it permits light to enter while maintaining the privacy of each room.

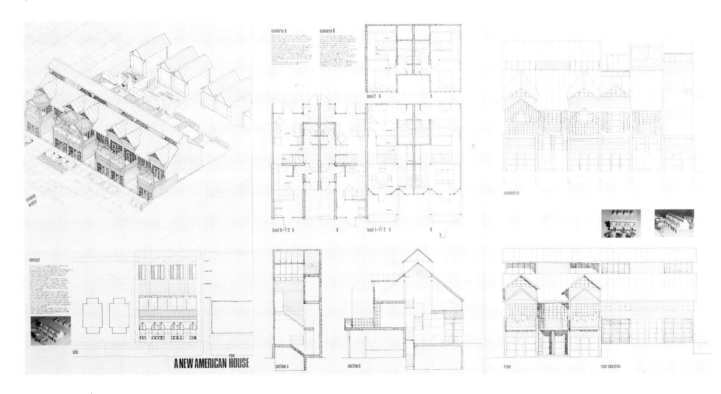

A NEW AMERICAN HOUSE

Michael Fifield

Tempe, Arizona

Zoning ordinances often attempt to segregate commercial from residential buildings, with the rationalization that different activities are incompatible. This practice has led to an environment lacking the qualities that make a city vibrant -- the everyday interaction of people performing different tasks. It is the richness and diversity of experience that transform a simple space into a special place. My solution integrates the houses' varied uses, both at the site plan and the unit levels, to insure needed privacy and enable physical and visual interaction to provide a stimulating environment.

This site plan concept uses a courtyard scheme to form a semi-public pedestrian street integrating residential and office activities. The offices front the pedestrian street, their separate public entrances further defined by the cantilevered second floor element. Additional coding devices such as window treatment, materials, steps and walls distinguish this public area from the private, residential portions of the community. The residential areas use familiar elements that convey "house" - such as chimney, roof, windows and trellis -- as abstracted images and not simply to simulate elements of the neighborhood.

Each unit's "L" shaped plan forms a semi-private courtyard which fronts the "pedestrian street' and acts as a transitional device to the residential area. A private door at the intersection of the "L's" legs allows entry at the middle of the unit, eliminating unnecessary hallways and providing access to all areas of the unit without passing through one activity zone to get to another. Spatial variety and richness are achieved by using all architectural elements (floors, walls, columns, windows and light, and ceilings and roofs) to their fullest potential.

Energy concerns are addressed by the absence of windows on the north wall. The closets, bookcases, bathrooms, and kitchen cabinets on the north wall act as energy and sound buffers. A two story living space adds volume to the unit, making it appear much larger than it really is.

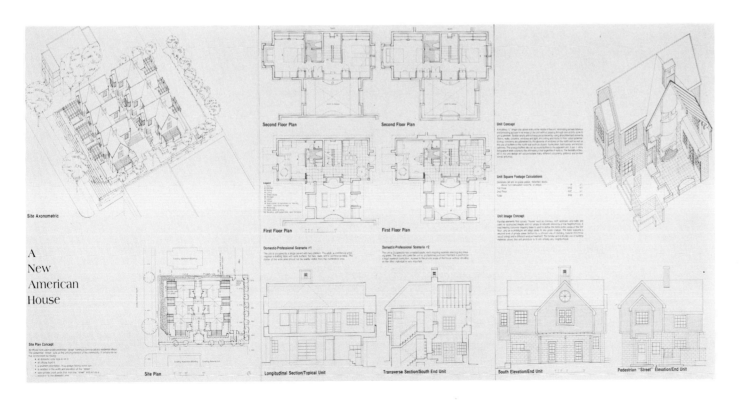

A New American House

Naomi and Amos Yoran
Karen Markison

Pittsburgh, Pennsylvania

Our challenge was to create a house type which integrates important new features with highly valued attributes of the outmoded "American Dream."

Traditional attributes we considered indispensable were ownership of, and direct link to, land; proximity to one's car; the "sanctity" of the private bathroom; and a clear separation and buffering of the private domain from the public area.

Newer qualities we wanted our design to provide included an enhancement of the personal space to accommodate varied activities, greater separation between private living spaces, and clear internal and external distinction between the residential and the workplace sections of the house. We thought the design should encourage greater interaction between adjacent households. House groupings should share facilities. We wanted a defensible outdoor space between the house and the public domain and increased capability for environmental control and utilization of recoverable energy resources. We considered the following elements essential: integrated expedients for personalization, upgrading and expansion, and supports for anticipated evolution of the house, particularly shape adaptations and technological innovations.

Our solution is a row-house unit with the basic form of a half doughnut. This morphology provides a number of fundamental features.

One enters the unit at its center through a court or patio, rather than the typical access from the external facade. Consequently, circulation is confined to a central service/circulation core; the two sides are freed to assume any role, to adapt, even to expand; the street front can be minimized without compromising room sizes; and a spatial hierarchy distinguishes the public from the private domain.

With the rooftop, the design provides a two-tiered southern exposure. The house can be rotated 180° with respect to the south with no loss in solar exposure. This enables designers to determine geographic orientation independently of socio-spatial orientation.

Two grouping topologies are possible. Units can be built in procession to maintain complete privacy of the entrance patios. Or, two units can be combined into a "whole doughnut" to create a shared, defensible inner court which can be used in many ways: external extension of workplaces, protected area for children, semi-private meeting place, or shared atrium (if enclosed).

We reapportioned space, allocating two-thirds to personal spaces. The reduced common area is compensated by including a sunspace, incorporating visual space - extending cues and providing a wide interface with the private outdoors.

Spaces are designed (in terms of size, proportions, adjacencies, window and door locations) to accommodate the furnishings of many different types of households. Two extreme cases are illustrated: a two-child, single-parent family with the parent having a psychology clinic; and a two-adult household with an artist's studio and rather flamboyant lifestyles.

As a statement of our belief in the future shaping of the built environment, we have introduced the first phase of an environmental support structure designed to take on solar collecting devices (photovoltaics) as well as wind and sun screening. Eventually we foresee this superstructure enveloping the entire building to create a controlled inner environment, which frees the present envelope to become a lightweight, adaptable space divider.

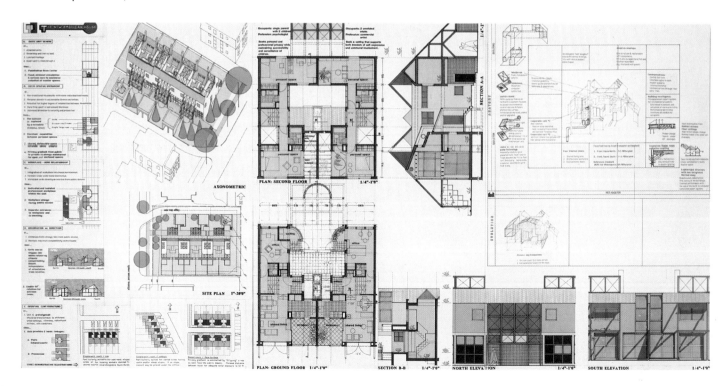

Marta Gutman
Michelle Kayon

Two distinct yet paired propositions structure the development of this New American House. First, the project exhibits qualities of a city in miniature; second, it satisfies the emerging housing needs of combined professional and domestic lives. The project design encourages choice and interpretation through use.

The courtyard-garden, jointly held by all the tenants, controls the site organization and suggests several uses. It could be a locus of small-scale commercial life, an outdoor gathering place, or small park where tenants can take the sun or meet their neighbors. For clients and office workers, the

Thomas Krahenbuhl
Deborah Norden

courtyard-garden fulfills the distributive and social functions of a lobby. By linking the offices spatially and visually, the front porch-arcade supports this reading. Other tectonic elements, such as the pergola, the herb gardens, and a community building, further articulate the site with their variety of scale and function. Parking is situated below the community building and the rear gardens.

The design of the prototype-cluster reconciles the diverse requirements of adjacent home and workplace. It guarantees the privacy of two non-traditional families while connecting their separate worlds to a more public

Eugene Sparling

New York, New York

realm. Two units share a small scale entry patio which opens to the courtyard-garden and contains entrances to the houses and offices. While the patio unites the two houses around a common center, it distinguishes each house from its office. The building massing and section emphasize this distinction. Moreover, the patio and office zone face the large courtyard-garden and separate the private part of the residence from the most public part of the site.

While the cluster clearly differentiates the residence and the workplace, the unit design remains flexible. For instance, tenants can use either of two

Honorable Mention

entries to their residence as their front door. The skylit, double-height stair hall creates two paths on the first floor and perceptually expands the compact plan. All the rooms have distinct architectural characters yet can be used and furnished in different ways: a bedroom can function as a study, the living room and dining room are interchangeable, and the office rooms can accommodate a variety of professional activities. To assure internal privacy, the house is organized in broadly defined functional areas, such as living spaces on the first floor and bedrooms on the second, and clearly defined circulation spaces join the various rooms. There are also several outdoor spaces: the shared patio, the private garden, and the second story terrace.

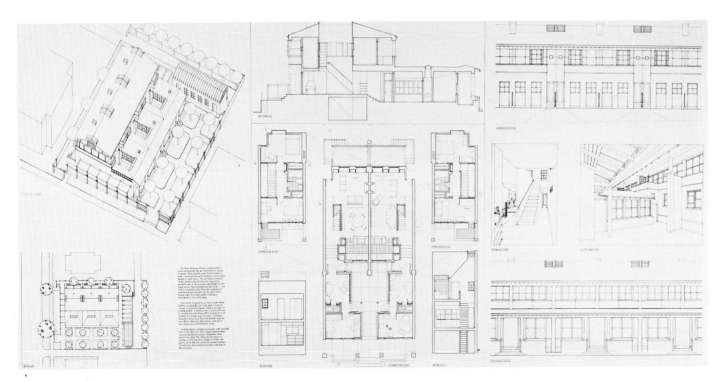

Patrick George

San Francisco, California

The panels that form the triptych consist of three full sheets of printmaking paper (22½" x 30") on which have been printed images from 31 etched zinc plates. The plates have been etched using such techniques as hard-ground, soft-ground, and aquatint. They are printed in different combinations and arrangements to produce the transformation of images from left to right in the triptych. In each panel the paper was run through the press a number of times with different plates each time to achieve the overlay effect.

The fundamental idea of this design is represented by the three windows which change from rectangular to triangular to circular. These windows border two worlds, but instead of looking out, they look into the realm of the mind. To design a truly New American House you must change your thinking on houses: deepen it, elaborate upon it, and infuse it with transcendent meaning. New forms are not enough; an evolution of consciousness is necessary, as is represented by the changing geometry of the windows. The window elements and the size of their openings are proportioned according to the golden rectangle.

The metaphysical process begins as the window of the first panel focuses on the Magician who manipulates the four symbols of the tarot. These relate to the four elements, the four suits, and the four architectural typologies, and there is a mingling of all the meanings which these symbols represent. In a sense, the Magician is also an architect, but fundamentally he is an alchemist who will transmute these elements and their corresponding meanings into the form of a house.

The focus of the second panel is the Rose, the symbol of the unconscious mind which expresses itself through the heart's emotions. The Empress from the tarot symbolizes the door and imagination; the Emperor symbolizes the window and reason. Together they are the archetypal "users" of the house, and they oversee the process by which the architectural elements are endowed with subconscious meaning and emotion. As with the Magician, the background to the Empress and the Emperor consists of an urban view which complements their individual meanings.

In the third panel the house has been created and the limitations of physical form have been transcended. The traditional architecture of grey, ancient columns lingers, supporting the dice of chance. The key to the house is Magritte's flaming key, as if taken directly from the alchemist's hearth wherein all the ideas and processes which led to the house were melded together with that metaphysical fire of truth and knowledge. The flame protects the house from the uninitiated. Last are the six thousand dollar bills which are framed by the final window -- money contrasted with meaning, as in the flaming key window. The viewer is left with a final mystery, its meanig to be found in the depths of that metaphysical house.

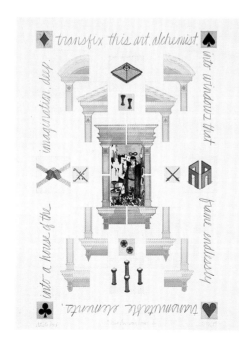
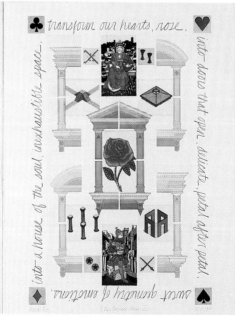
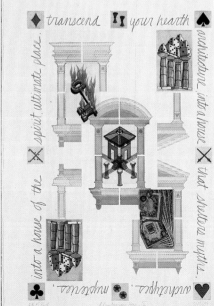

Michael Joyce

Brooklyn, New York

The most important goal in this design was to provide the sense of community important to non-nuclear families. The design was inspired by a two-up, two-down four-plex in Minneapolis, a building which has a strong feeling of involvement among the tenants, who are very similar to the people mentioned in the competition scenarios.

What fosters this communal environment in the four-plex is a common enclosed back hall, with a door and a window into each unit's kitchen. The hall is a natural place for casual encounters, borrowing things, watching each other's children, sharing advice and providing company, supplementing and enriching a non-nuclear family.

In A New American House, these features are transferred to a more luxurious site, with outdoor areas and a garage. The common back yard becomes the back hall. The residents park their cars and walk past each other's private courtyards and kitchen doors. This is not as communal as the hallway in the four-plex, but the yard is enclosed, so only the residents would likely be there.

The units are zoned into public (work) and private (household) areas. This permits the household to operate without interruption to the work space. When clients are not present, the work space can open up to the private area.

Visitors to the work area enter through the more formal entrance which relates to the street.

The living space overlooks a private outdoor courtyard. A formal living room and a kitchen-dining room, which may act as a family room, are separated by a hallway. This separation is necessary during long Minnesota winters when much time is spent indoors. The bedrooms are planned as two separate suites with private baths. The shape of the attic enables expansion into a loft configuration.

The site was kept as one large, uncluttered, green lawn to satisfy the Minnesota preference for open space. The buildings are intended to look friendly and homey, with that stucco and brick aesthetic so common in South Minneapolis. In time, with a few years growth of trees and ivy, the project will fade into the neighborhood and be a compatible addition to the street. The buildings "point" towards each other to create a visual whole, an implied arch over the common yard. The tall attics provide the scale of the adjacent buildings, and the street facade reflects the street plane.

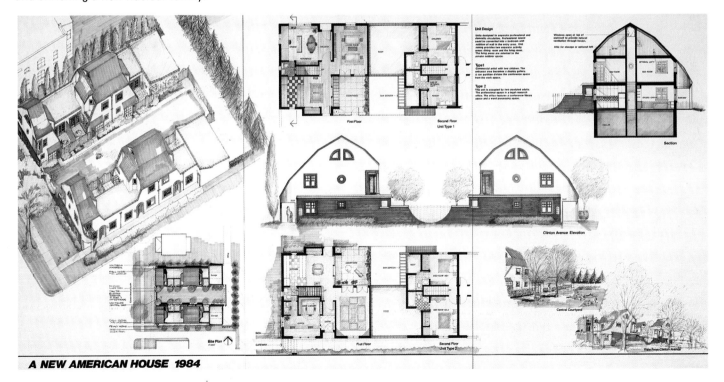

A NEW AMERICAN HOUSE 1984

Jim Shields
Harry Van Oudenallen

Milwaukee, Wisconsin

This design was developed with the understanding that the meaning of home is associated with images of independent, detached houses in a pastoral setting, and that these images are conditioned and consistently reinforced by magazines, television, movies, and other electronic media. The power of such conditioning is so vast that we are acknowledging its influence and have thus designed our New American Home with similar imagery and symbolism. In effect, we have created a collective sharing of the critical parts of "house" which makes this symbolism possible.

Whereas traditional housing stresses square footage and numbers of spaces, we have stressed volume and adaptable space use. Whereas traditional housing defines space explicitly through the use of walls, we have fostered spatial ambiguity, allowing for spatial definition in response to user preferences. Whereas traditional housing labels space use absolutely, we see the need for flexibility over time, expanding and contracting space as unexpected needs may arise. In our design, gross space is no longer the vehicle by which Americans can fulfill the need to territorialize, to imprint, or express their identity. Instead, our design illustrates the ten meaningful parts of "house" necessary to fulfill these needs for both the non-traditional and the traditional American Homebuyer.

We have established ten design responses to meaning in housing for the American Homebuyer:

The Gable: symbol of singular ownership, provides for private entry and establishes the center of the house,

The Carport and Gate: allow for the expression of one's relation with, and attitude toward, the car,

The Front Yard and Porch: a controlled semi-public area ready for further personalization,

The Chimney: expressive of the warmth and security of home, the fireplace provides heat and comfort--it is the heart,

Add-Ins: additional room and hallway over coffered ceiling and completion of upper decks could provide expansion without increased volume,

The Fence: beautiful fences make beautiful neighbors,

Wings of Rooms: L-shaped spaces for light from two sides define exterior space and make interior space feel larger,

Tall Ceiling/Living Space: kinesthetic experience through volumetric variety,

The Office/Studio/Workshop: living and working in the same place - "I am my own boss,"

The Estate: collective massing plus shared gates, entry, and drive provide convenience and elegance in living.

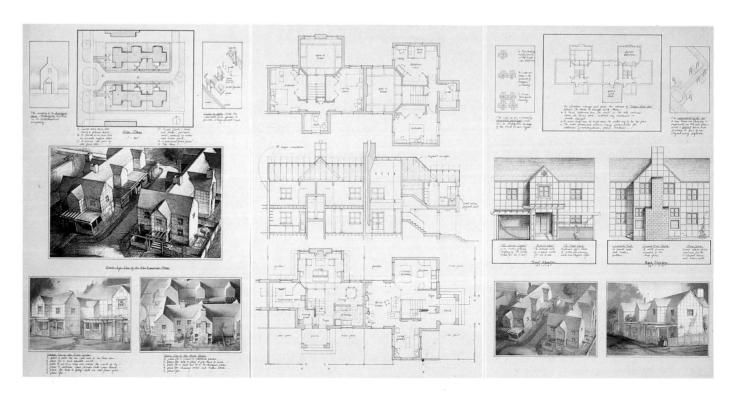

Ross Chapin

Langley, Washington

The neighborhood context for this project was an important consideration in my design approach. By re-creating in a new way the traditional form and massing common to many houses of the area, this design helps to restore the "fabric" of the neighborhood. The house cluster does not stand alone but, rather, tries to be a "good neighbor."

In a city where buildings are close together, usable outdoor space is critical. Spaces merely left between buildings are rarely used. In this design, building clusters are placed in relation to one another and to neighboring buildings to create a kind of "outdoor room." This space is protected yet open to the activity on the street. The residents will probably use and enjoy the space because it is in the sun and feels secure. The surrounding buildings look on, and hedges, fencing and clear entryways enhance the sense of common ownership and territory, making the space defensible for crime control. Staggering the buildings to create usable space also insures that no building is in the shade of another; each can have maximum solar exposure. The shaded, outdoor spaces to the north are walkways and transition areas. The parking area is another "room" that could also be used for games. It is close to the household entryways, but does not infringe upon them.

People who choose to work at home need their work space differentiated from their personal space. This design achieves that by providing separate professional and personal entries on either side of the building. At the same time, the workplace is closely connected to the personal dwelling space within the unit plan.

As living space becomes tighter and people live more closely together, privacy becomes more important. Each of these house units are arranged on three levels, creating several zones of privacy. The plan itself can be adapted to a variety of household types and uses.

From an economic standpoint, the form and plan of the house clusters are relatively simple and easy to build, making them affordable in today's market.

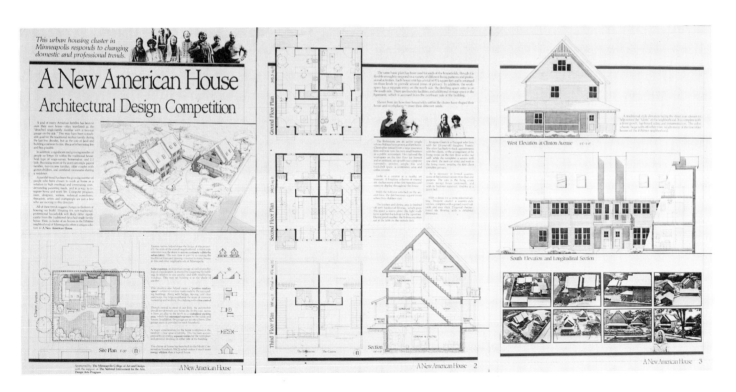